AF247574

# AN EXILE FROM SILENCE

## POEMS TO GOD

## by Patricia Wilcox

ALEMBIC PRESS
ITHACA, NEW YORK 

A few of the poems in this book were previously published
in *Alembic* and *Roberson Poetry Annual*.

Alembic Press thanks the National Endowment for the Arts
for a grant that supported the publication of this book.

*Where practicable, poems continued on a second page are divided
between stanzas; the symbol † indicates that a stanza
has been interrupted for pagination.*

Printed in the United States of America     1 2 3 4 5

**Library of Congress Cataloging in Publication Data**

Wilcox, Patricia, 1932 –
    An exile from silence.

    Includes index.
    I. Title.
PS3573.I417E9          811'.54          81-12828
ISBN 0-934184-09-7 (hardcover)          AACR2
ISBN 0-934184-10-0 (paperback)

FOR

*Dr. Maria Moulton-Barrett*

# *Introduction*

On a recent visit to Washington, D.C., I stood on the steps of the Mall entrance to the National Gallery of Art for the first time, gazing up at the lofty portico, spellbound: the massive columns rose with such magnanimous ease and power the distant roof seemed in another, metaphysical, world. My companion stepped near and said: "Now imagine what it must have been like to live in a culture that worshiped in temples like that."

After reading this book, I am left feeling as I felt standing on those steps: humbled by awe, and ennobled.

"There is no element more conspicuously absent from contemporary poetry than nobility," wrote Wallace Stevens in *The Necessary Angel.* "Pareto's epigram that history is a cemetery of aristocracies easily becomes another: that poetry is a cemetery of nobilities. For the sensitive poet, conscious of negations, nothing is more difficult than the affirmations of nobility and yet there is nothing that he requires of himself more persistently." Patricia Wilcox is a poet of vast learning in the "cemetery of nobilities." *A Public and Private Hearth*, her second collection of poems and the first to be published (by the Bellevue Press in 1978), shows her to be a poet of intense and intelligent mindfulness, with a semantically rich but plain-spoken free verse style. A lively mix of sophisticated rhetoric and informal, idiomatic accents, the poetry in that book can hit notes on the emotional scale from effervescent joy to holy terror. Satire is its golden mean and mode of equilibrium. Whether ridiculing the dolor so fashionable in contemporary writing or the facile discussion by the mass media of death and dying, Wilcox's satirical poems scintillate witty, epigrammatic lines, the mark of a poet who finds in thought poetry's greatest challenges and pleasures of achievement. Not "notes from underground" but rather "memos from indoors," the poems in *A Public and Private Hearth* skirmish with the outside world's cruelty, corruption, and hypocrisy, holding at bay all that threatens personal integrity. Even when she writes to praise moments and beings who nullify her bleakest conclusion—that the enemy is already within—Wilcox refuses poetic simplicities: the lyrical impulse bends to her precision-mongering intellect; the result is imagery as beautifully phrased as it is complexly thoughtful. The same sure craft, passionate intelligence and leavening wit found in her previous book are present in this one, but in these poems the stakes have been raised to an unheard-of risk. The poet of *A Public and Private Hearth* begins *An Exile from Silence* as a person on the verge of a radical transformation.

In the summer of 1979 Patricia Wilcox read *The Self-Embodiment of God* by Thomas J.J. Altizer. An atheist, she was inspired by the words of that "death of God" theologian to begin a sequence of poems addressed to God. The result is poetry of awesome dramatic impact and intellectual power.

These poems enact her confrontation with the theologian's concepts, testing them against her own experience and thought. The poems are not ruminations. Wilcox feels her thoughts in a way that most poets today do not, because she believes that poetry is a way to think and that thinking is a matter of life or death for "that to/ us once baldly called *The Soul* — a sort of/ public-private hearth roaring with besieged/ mind." As that definition from her previous book suggests, faith and doubt have long warred in Wilcox's mind, which characteristically turns to irony for a dialectical truce, at once embracing and warding off the spirit of negation. Her provisional conclusions are necessarily grim in *A Public and Private Hearth*, as one would expect of a poet who empathizes so completely with the archetypal human sufferer, a portion of whose lot falls to us all. In a poem found on that book's final pages, "Nothing Taxes Resources Like Confronting Genuine Grief," she conjures "the madman who/ is himself a desert," who if we let him "will finish our tattered/ faith in water." When Eliphaz, Bildad and Zophar came to succor Job, the depth of his grief compelled them to sit silently in the ashes for a week. Our empathy would require as much:

> Can we make this nightmare visit, stiffen
> yet let everything go? March as blind ministrants
> with our lamps unto the chamber where light
> is mockery? Can we make up the sacred cast of
> characters and dance as stone angels over the
> single and many crypts? Can we go down to it,
> many become one, community a gleaming chain of
> pure descent that weds forever gain to loss?
>
> *Holy madman, we are the same!*

An *Exile from Silence* starts from that identification with misery. The first poem names God in images of dying, decay and pain; the second calls Him to account:

> Judgment hangs above this hideout
> where I count my miseries.
> Not mine alone. All misery calls.
>
> Are you, then, misery?
> Pure other, exiled from self,
> can you feel? Oh God, God, are we
> the ache in your invisible bones,
> the tearing muscle, the mindless
> cancer cells?
>
> God, you murderer, you scapegrace,
> MALINGERER!                                    (9/16/79)

The shifts in tone here are emotional lightning, from the stern opening to surprising tenderness for God's imagined plight to the swift taking-back of sympathy with impassioned denunciation. The silence that follows her rage is a changed silence, a charged silence. In the poem dated 10/18/79 anger rebounds, her judgment of God becomes self-judgment:

> And what a laugh! I have sought goodness,
> the merest whisper, the voiceless, delicate,
> something urged vulnerable in the hoarsest
> drunken voices, a vapor of Call out of putrefaction.
> Kill it! Kill it quick before it knows itself,
> before it speaks a single irre-vocable.
> Weep, Rachel, before grief exceeds
> the hope of weeping.
>
> Get down to it! You took my child,
> made my womb a shroud, binding me over
> to perfect grief. Ten times over I'd die
> for his restoration. It doesn't move you.
> You teach me *I am not.*

Altizer's theological terms are touchstones in these poems. One need not pre-digest the theology to understand the poetry. The terms are not foreign: *silence*; *presence*; *judgment*; the *I am* that answers the *I AM* and faces *I am not.* The poems in the first third of the book establish the meaning of these concepts for Wilcox as she argues them in the light and dark of her soul. By 12/7/79 a note of resolution sounds in her discourse:

> Oh God, I wonder if you alone
> are coherent self, shed of all accidents
> of personality to which we are hapless heirs.
>
> Let judgment fall upon me.
> I will my self. I say *I.*
> I will obliteration of this I: I say *I am not.*
> Much selfhood sings within me.
> Silence surrounds it with a holy circle.
> What I am is hidden.
> I cannot even know the self I utter.
> It is poured out forever
> into silence.
> It will not return.
> I give it up.

The silence by which we are made aware of our alienation from God and feel our estrangement from nature becomes for Wilcox the way into another state of mind. In his essay "The New Consciousness" from *Zen and the Birds of Appetite*, Thomas Merton describes two types of consciousness available to us in the West: the predominant Cartesian consciousness and an alternative, metaphysical, consciousness that overcomes the religious dead-end to which the former inevitably leads. He summarizes what brought about the "death of God" theology this way: "Cartesian thought began with an attempt to reach God as object by starting from the thinking self. But when God becomes object, he sooner or later 'dies,' because God as object is ultimately unthinkable." The Cartesian consciousness experiences this "death" as a liberation, but still feels trapped in itself and tries to break out in "fellowship," in *I-Thou* meetings that free it from the *I-it* relationships dictated by its perception of others as objects. The alternative consciousness, Merton asserts, "starts not from the thinking and self-aware subject but from Being ontologically seen to be beyond and prior to the subject-object division." The self-aware subject that emerges from this consciousness, unlike the Cartesian self, is not absolute, but "a provisional self-construction which exists, for practical purposes, only in a sphere of relativity. Its existence has meaning in so far as it does not become fixated or centered upon itself as ultimate, learns to function not as its own center but 'from God' and 'for others.' "

The poems in this book evolve a religious sensibility grounded in this type of consciousness. The self-liberation that Wilcox experiences through her "dialogue with silence" is not the unequivocal conversion of one who embraces a "plan of salvation," but is a dialectical faith, holding doubt within itself, requiring day by day renewal in actuality—the giving up of self to silence and to the "sphere of relativity" where the self exists as one among others, bound by caring. Late in the book when Wilcox has firmly taken hold of this faith, she is severely shaken by the murder of the son of close friends. She must solace them by embracing their hopelessness, at the same time asserting her new-found hope:

> Shattered by presence,
> I bow to dull daily caring, to hope
> that can't sing but plugs ahead,
> too tired and dusty for the name.
> Hell, what is hope?
> A great interminable foolishness? (10/7/80)

*An Exile from Silence* is replete with poems that focus on the relations of the self with others, poems written about particular relationships and poems that probe the dynamics of relationships in general, the self's need and dread of others. In the course of the book Wilcox's death-longing disappears into a longing to give herself away. Merton asserts a cause-effect connection between the non-Cartesian, metaphysical consciousness and the giving up of the self: "The metaphysical intuition of Being is an intuition of a *ground of openness*, indeed of a kind of ontological openness and an infinite generosity which communicates itself to everything that is. 'The good is diffusive of itself,' or 'God is love.' Openness is not something to be acquired but a radical gift that has been lost and must be recovered."

I believe Wilcox would add that expressing the gift once it has been recovered is extremely difficult. She is chronically beset by feelings of cynicism and self-loathing, is let down or falls from that state of grace, and must work back toward it, with the help of others. (This book is dedicated to one we may assume has been of special importance in her striving to be a living expression of that openness, her therapist.) The poem dated 10/9/80 speaks of her chronic self-doubts and her dependence on others who depend on her:

> Ashamed of my deformities, open sores,
> bungling hands, shuffling gait —
> I should help somebody?
>
> I'd have left long since
> except for these monsters of suffering,
> who deserve my mirroring self
> set before their shameless continuing
> in spite of, in spite of...
>
> Dumped into bed each night
> this carcass, little abler
> than just needful to haul
> its own sludge across
> the criminal expanse of a day!
>
> I, the needy, pouring out
> what I don't have. I, the leper,
> loving, beloved in my turn,
> trying not to waste it.

About the time Patricia Wilcox was reading Thomas J.J. Altizer's *The Self-Embodiment of God*, I was reading *The Illusion of Technique* by William Barrett, a book that finds in the works of Wittgenstein, Heidegger and William James a synthesized perspective that could rescue modern consciousness by a route corresponding to the one Merton describes and which this book maps. "The statement 'I believe,'" Barrett argues, "can only be uttered as a prayer. In the beginning was the prayer." He concludes his discussion of William James with another pertinent apothegm: "Faith is not affirmation of a proposition independent of the will; it is the act of will in its prayer." In the penultimate poem of this book Wilcox writes:

No visionary dreaming God everywhere,
I bring you here,

taste you in my own mouth,
touch you in my own body.                              (3/29/81)

Interestingly, I found in Barrett's book the agenda for any poetry that would aspire today to affirm a nobility equal to the nobilities of the past:

> Two centuries ago, a century ago, men thought of themselves as the masters of history; today we are more likely to think of ourselves as its victims. The literature of the twentieth century is largely a lamentation for ourselves as victims. And in nothing are we more victims than in this: that we have to cope with the same life as humankind in the past but without its most potent means of doing so. We cannot will back a faith that has been lost. We shall have to live back into that way of being in whose ambience the religious once drew breath.

*An Exile from Silence* shows us what it feels like to do exactly that. The essential meaning of the book is beyond the theology that inspired it, in the mystery of the poems, which can only be read and read again. I'm convinced that these poems are destined to find the great audience due them. The book's most appreciative readers will be those who cannot abide the various and conflicting certainties of the many religions available to them. These readers will be eternally grateful to Patricia Wilcox for helping them to live their lives without those certainties; for showing them that it is possible for them to be among the faithful after all.

*David Dayton*
*Editor and Publisher of Alembic Press*
*July 1981*

# An Exile from Silence

*The presence of speech embodies an exile from silence, an exile from that silence which is simply and only itself. That exile is real, actually and audibly real, and we realize it whenever we either listen or speak.*

> —Thomas J.J. Altizer
> in *The Self-Embodiment of God*

*Genuine solitude is a voyage into the interior, but it is a voyage which culminates in a loss of our interior, a loss reversing every manifest or established center of our interior so as to make possible the advent of a wholly new but totally immediate world.*

> —Thomas J.J. Altizer
> in *Total Presence*

God is in the flowerpot
where the African violet
is at long last dying.

Without gender, without charity
for Marie's worries
or any lone scratching for survival
in a wasted soil,

God is being cut away
with the dead limbs of the maple,
swept up and mulched with the leaves.

Who needs this dialectical excuse,
Tom, this verbose seduction, this
conjurer's act, these stern meditations
upon stony words from an old book?

God is in Mario's bad back
and in Gordon's, in the work
they are kept from
because, says Doctor Arthur—
another friend with a bad back—
the human back has not evolved
properly and anyhow is put to wrong use
by moderns.

God, you are on my back again!
Thanks to Tom. Weak and ill-used
as the others, it cries out into the silence.

Judgment hangs above this hideout
where I count my miseries.
Not mine alone. All misery calls.

Are you, then, misery?
Pure other, exiled from self,
can you feel? Oh God, God, are we
the ache in your invisible bones,
the tearing muscle, the mindless
cancer cells?

God, you murderer, you scapegrace,
MALINGERER!

You of the awesome bad conscience,
today I drink gall with Amos, while
the ghosts of skeletal children
welcome me to the long festering grave.

I am not up to this.
I am at the center of this,
with you, God,
naming.

Actual?
I insist upon you, silence.

You wooed me beside my father's
new red cracked grave
where all the wilderness of rural
gulped me, that hither real
always at my vitals.

You called me in her perfumed
and corseted chatter,
my mother always departing.

And oh did I call that neighbor
*simple?* Raw dirt farmer-deacon,
head flung backwards
in defiance, bawling a hymn?

Tomatoes glisten in white
market baskets on the bed
of an old truck,

bent effort in each globe
going, calling,
as color held in a hand speaks.

And I am crouched,
I am coiled,
I am clenched like a fist to hear

what my father heard,
cocking his great head
against wide Georgia sky,
in petulant séance with the land.

Everything drives me crazy —
my menopausal body, the whole bleeding
business of being female.

What decent message from that bustle
of powder and prissiness? Nothing
I can hear or speak. Only Daddy,
overwhelming as his road machinery.
My little brothers yelled; I'd squeeze
them hungrily to my body, that terrible
tight-to-the-skin desire, chortling
joy in them, hoping to grow a penis?
Negating that hunger, I abandoned them.

One has flown, or was shot down
in flight. We don't know. God!
The unspeakable guilt and grief.
They will say his mother is being
punished, and as I dared join
in his mothering so am I. On goes
the dismal chatter, the soap-opera
mothers. When they stop for breath,
three million Cambodians starve me to death.

Shouldn't the newspapers be printed
in blood drawn from the veins
of the fortunate? Oh vile splendor
of you losing mothers, teach
me how to chatter.

God, God, why do you leave me?
In my rite of mourning, I still
play and sing the old hymns,
negating this dark country of my exile,

here where you tease me
like a narcissistic lover, leaving
me in these rags of grace, each note
my fingers shakily sound comfort's
dull echo.

This ache, God. Does God leave God?
At the mysterious heart of anguish
a silence loathing its own void
rips the very covenant of language.
Who are these people? I do not know them,
though I sing back to Whitman, to Hawthorne,
to Melville. I have lived so long with death
it is my one clear desire. Give me silence!
Take me back, leave me unsaid. Home
is exile, a grotesque vision of unclean
lips feeding upon their own progeny.

And what a laugh! I have sought goodness,
the merest whisper, the voiceless, delicate,
something urged vulnerable in the hoarsest
drunken voices, a vapor of Call out of putrefaction.
Kill it! Kill it quick before it knows itself,
before it speaks a single irre-vocable.
Weep, Rachel, before grief exceeds
the hope of weeping.

Get down to it! You took my child,
made my womb a shroud, binding me over
to perfect grief. Ten times over I'd die
for his restoration. It doesn't move you.
You teach me *I am not.*

When I dreamed, sang, spoke,
demanded abiding, you left me.

Drunken slut, desperado, I sang
how the darkness deepened.
It deepened. Nothing stayed.
Silence!

Funny, God, this long losing
in the wilderness, wandering
among known strangers, intimacy
a sting, a reproach, a harassment.

And how loving failed most, becoming
its other, until voice stammered, broke,
until I stared into the void
of a single word.

Now, those plain singers
in the one-room church, I doubt
they understood *jasper walls* and *mansions*,
but they well understood, God, their lack
of understanding, singing anyhow.

Tasting pine and mud of this past
with me, with me now, God,
old porcupine me, *I am*, waddles
on down that lonesome road,
where *I am not*, where strains of
tattering hymns implore nothingness,
assault silence.

Skunk self. Eau de Charnel.
Skewered with beatitude, crying
ABIDE WITH ME! Ho, ho.

This weekend a pair of logicians!
Like Mississippi riverboat gamblers,
tight in their spiffy clothes,
all knotted, buttoned, vested in,

they played with *John believes*
*that Tom believes that Bob is drunk*,
speaking in symbols and formal proofs,
sallying in lofty rhetoric, full of
romance, gesture and jest.

My God, it was a fast game! Graceful
duelists, their beautiful closed faces
seemed made for enhancing scars.

I liked this phrase: *believing true*,
thinking of the mind's bedazzlements
in Moore, *like Gieseking playing Scarlatti*.
I thought how pride and humility
go linked in such acts,
when the best instruments
descend to the lowliest work.
To know such danger
over so small a matter!
To give one's life to grammar!

What a lovely and lovable war.

If I am, God, only when I stand
alone under judgment, calling
to presence all I would escape,

then only do I truly stand forth,
single upon a field, a wonder to myself.

These are my words.
These are my deeds.
These are my crimes.
Here my strength, my weakness.
I am.

Only from here can this criminal
continue in crime, this patient
act in illness, this mother nurture
and reject, this wife love and turn
away from loving, this friend
be treacherous and true.

Here, God, I am easy
in my uneasiness.
*This shaking keeps me steady*
Roethke sang.

I see my son's brute innocence,
its present beauty from the distance
much grief and dying measures
within me, from the judgment and silence
come after life and death hung balanced,
when *I am* answered *I AM*
and I faced *I am not.*

A world without you, God, is not
a world. I am tired, tired.
Near the riverside, I cannot
lay down my burdens.

Come to me, children, unborn
before you answer in blood
that bloody event when a hard mothering
screamed and muscled you from
the softest cradle of silence.
I say to you, cry out *I am*
with the brute force of nameless naming.
God, am I born yet? Ever?

"Closer...than breathing,
...nearer than hands and feet"?
Once I lay, mute, my babe upon
my wrinkled belly, as though we joined
in the fetal fluid of first creation,
rocking silently, curled together
in an utter moment, finally safe.

Was it not you, God, who held us?
What mother can say this? It belongs
to silence, to questioning without end.
Door and door, God, birth and death,
opening, opening...

I did not hear.
I did not see.
I did not hope.
I did not fear.

Babe and mother coalescing,
a rocking in silence.

How some of the greatest hymns
appall me now!:
*A mighty fortress is our God —*
*God, the omnipotent! King, who ordainest —*

What has silence to do
with such force and volume?
I will not call you *Lord.*
I will not call you *Master, King, et al.*

You fail as I fail, as people fail,
enter powerlessness without return.
Onward Christian soldiers?
No. You always double back
to gather the skewed bodies
on the gouged mud of the field.
What stake have we in victory,
obtuse blabbermouth!
In us questions whisper
in bewilderment
after vicious judgment has been done;
after the solemn and sordid treaty,
we bed with the bleak,
unhusbanded,
unchilded,
living out hard losses,

and visit in shock
palsied hands, the haunting
wastes where,

crazed by mutual murder,
we miss legs and arms.

Mute white crosses
ordered in the disarray
shrilled by silence.
Ticks of horror bursting with blood!

Always emptying yourself of yourself,
not lord but servant,
judge only as witness
of judgment and in that judgment
as judged. Everywhere is *I AM* becoming *I AM NOT.*
Even in Luther's fantasy,
in the appalling martial hymns,
in the young soldier's tender face
bemused by dreams of valor,
before and after death.

Thinking of Conrad's *significant
nobodies*, I come to this page
a scavenger, not wanting my life
except to give it away somehow,

for stripped of shrillness,
stripped to the shell
that can hear only
and can hear its own silence
as pure response, I crave

the self of another,
my blind friend, his gay charity
that rings and echoes through me

there where he stands
in darkness within the party's garish
circle, on the ledge of himself,
speaking a life dearer than his own,

performing without light
an orchestration, sounds as a tale
that can be told, a continuing.

Bob, lover of accents, do you hear
also our silence? In your great hall
of night, our words must flower like fireworks,
each flare, each fading.

It must be so. I see it in your face,
that unbelievably joyous face,
night's antic child,
God's child, my child
whose child I am,

here where we stand, Bob,
mute and garrulous,
grief and grace,
on the ledge of ourselves.

Dear God, what am I,
spider and fly, devouring
and devoured in one cramped motion?

Don't let me bog down in the domestic.

This hearth I so protect
should blaze out and singe me
into keener sensibility.
Creaks and shadows—bah!
Lead me into big trouble.
Give me fears worth fearing.
I am dead from prudence, reek of safety.

I'm deep in news items and dirty dishes,
tripping to the grocery, scouring
my damnable teeth—all the sweet quotidian
mess that lulls me,
behind whose clutter
lie terror, death, madness.

Are you in that dank corner, too,
hiding? Okay, YOU, put up your dukes!
It is late, and as Jurgen put it,
"It is not fair." I sink with Cabell
in the romance of quicksand pathos.
Gum operations and cancer. Hair,
weight, cosmetics and tampons.
Wine and cheese, God help me!

Everywhere are hungerers.
I hunger for an end to all this
paltry hungering.

Torn, Oh God, between the light
that hides the dark
and the dark that despairs of light,
torn, say, between Jane
and Joseph, two loves of mine,

I wait in the silence.
Who will take my hand today, God?

There is chill in her gaiety.
There is blood-warmth in his gloom.

Ha! Comes a vision: my cynic Pole
embraces, kisses his ideal English woman.
In the moment they marry.
He is gay. She glooms.
Out of an old sea chest
he takes his boyhood dream.
She turns away to a grief
deeper than any sea he sailed,
polar to his tropic joy.

I speak, my God, of perfect loss.

To these actors, add my mask,
of the wordy wedding guest
meant for such marriages,
ink with paper.

Will you attend?
Bring wine,
presence?

With gauds of death, yellow leaves
and wet black boughs, the year
relinquishes the old business of growth
for a sleep of snow,

and, rather than sleep, I call
to presence my old friend, Ali,
our fierce visit, how in it her loving
would not be silenced,

whose shaming tears for my grief
were fisted angrily from her lucid,
wearing face, defying my wordless,
tearless chill, the sleet
about my heart.

God, do you send such tinder
to the sullen hearth? Send Ali,
a lady of fallen sparrows, to break,
erode, melt before my very eyes?

How still I grew beneath the soft
rain of her tears!

Here I gladly waste my syllabled
breath for her tears wrenched
out of silence to the self's damnation.
Water burns. Good erupts out of evil.
Who cares about years?

Against another shrill principle
niftily positioned
to whitewash greed and tyranny,

I close my ears. I hear instead
my anomalous ones, the fallen,
the sleepless, the desperate,
called to presence
of the greatest anomaly of all.

I want your jitters, curses, calamities.
Here at the center all is agenda.
Say it out! Hurry up before I decide
to cower in my bed for a month.

Farmers must take advantage of spring.
Next week I may betray us, so tell me,
my lovely, why did you turn on yourself,
try to wrest *I am* from *I AM?*

And, you, what is it? You don't trust
me or anybody.

Give me the pure hellishness. I need
to take it straight. We need to curse,
shudder and cry together, to give up,

let silence cherish us.

God how I have loved my
beautiful dead sisters!
I have sucked at those
perfumed and softly gowned corpses.
I have given those shades
new bodies and worshiped my effigies.
My mouth is full of death.

I am entering my long terror.
I have been too stern to live.

Take away this dish, you
to whom anything can be spoken.
I want to dance as Sarah did,
sing and play the piano like Margaret,

or do nothing at all
in my own body. Be watchful.
Silent. Listen. Be.

I want the Kingdom Come
of sure mortality,
the careless death of a vegetable,
to be known as a carrot is,
something that comes and goes,
something edible
and equal to its nurture.

Help me give the brilliant dead girls
to silence. Little witch,
what a brew of sex and death
you stir!

Come, your feet are cracked, dirty
and bleeding. Come, your hand-me-down
dress is torn. Come, your forlorn heart
like an oceanic drum is beating, beating...
Come from your romance of sisters
†

to the terror you repeat . . .
The romance is the terror and will not
depart. In the dark of my silent childhood
I fell fathoms, screaming so that none
could hear, the silent scream of pride.

Help of the helpless,
give me a word.

Oh rest in silence!
Wait patiently for Amen and peace.
Come home, come home;
weary one, come home.

Silence calls me in Maria's
patient, intelligent loving.
*Listen to yourself*, she counsels.
Listen to silence.
Who told her that?

Will actual words rise
out of the noise and chatter,
when the body is bent
in the waiting mode?

Maria, my shrink!
So her kind are called in the tribe.
And so I tribally mock her,
naming what cannot be named,

what happened in the interstices
of our endless conversation,
the moments of sheer stun.

*He opened not his mouth.*

Maria and I speak, each to each,
from the cross of a calling.
We search and destroy each other,
then fall back into silence
where, dying in ruin,
we hear the jungle growing.

Conrad, you loved your heart of darkness!
It is the center that will hold,
if darkly.

For all our faith stretches us,
we remain apostles of the possible,
right? So here's your phrase-maker Auntie,
Don, joyless as Job,
feeling deprived and unequal,
courting, as usual, the nobodyness
of Aunt Emily, leaving my house
more than is prudent,

trying to love and fend off
at once, claiming the very edge.

If you, ward of my soul, dare
say *conversion* to me, I'll never
speak to you again! Nitwits
and rice are converted.
I wouldn't mind being a bag of rice,
given the times. But I ain't a nitwit;
no — as I regaled Maria —
I'm an Exceptional Child of 47 years!

Who could explain this?
It will never make consensus,
the sense being pretty comical.
Tom wrote a terrifying book
and seems to be hiding out,
maybe hoping nobody will take it seriously.

One more sad clown,
so we can trust him.
Hey, you clowns, World sez,
give us meaning we can market,
shove that camel of cowardice and greed
through the needle's eye of faith;
be a sexy and romantic fascist
or a leftist puritan,
anything tough and pleasant-tasting.

Hey, World, sez us,
here's a puzzle,
mystery if you will:

each life is a gamble
each tries to lose.

God, I used to fear failure.
Now I fear success.

Failing, we meet fellows
and warmly gripe and cavil.
We make the soup
and set the table,
visit with gratitude
what does not belong to us.

We go among the hale
as cripples with the privileges
of the begging cup.

I used to stomp, yell, cry a lot.
Rage now is too mighty for this.
And tears come hard,
the warmest blessing,
salt diamonds
evaporating all too quickly.

*Wrath*—a good old word
that still grabs my tongue—
also has room in you
where all has presence,
even ultimate shame.

We should not be ashamed to weep.
It is the proof of coming
to the edge of the self
where good can happen. It is the body's
happy reprieve from action
and calls for the act of another.
Helplessness helps so.

Tears and silence bond us
one to another.

My God, the snare and delusion
of it! – attempts on saintliness.
Here goes Aunt Patty, picking up
headaches and terrors in her apron,
as though it could hold without tearing.
Put this fat fool in restraints!
To "Help, love me!" make her deaf,
stop her in her tracks
to think it over, for love's a promise
we all enjoy making
but loathe keeping.

Well, it's not to be passed around
like pretzels, should be enduring
and endures best when reciprocal:
you hold me. I'll hold you.
Watch those turns!

In this, too, I sound
my own unsoundness, preserving my self
as first condition of helping.
Too middleaged and scared for much pleasure,
my greatest blessings are the pits
I've managed to skirt.

No Christ, I've yet a stake
in that nativity and passion.
You and I, God, sound each other,
go down to come back up,
being good for nothing.

Too much silence here for days.
I have gone attired in pathos,
stumbling against hard stones
of mortal fact — a near suicide,
loss of an old friend to utter death,
death finishing what distance began,

children trampled at a rock concert,
this last a vicious kick
to my frail stomaching of it all,
and, and...

Even so, something is won,
amazements in relief to living's killing,
the necessary violence we practice
if we don't jump ship, fall from the air,
suffocate under bodies avid for a high,
or die of even less natural causes.

Oh God, it seems we must love
the one self we can't be
if we begin the work of love at all.
Oh God, it seems we are our lone selves
never single. In a dream I was an Oriental man
ineffectually stabbing my dear husband,
and I was Caesar as my husband
bewildered in his several wounds,
and I was the eye hidden, back of
the camera, making a movie
meant for you, perhaps?

Oh God, I wonder if you alone
are coherent self, shed of all accidents
of personality to which we are hapless heirs.

Let judgment fall upon me.
I will my self. I say *I.*
I will obliteration of this I: I say *I am not.*
Much selfhood sings within me.
Silence surrounds it with a holy circle.
What I am is hidden.
I cannot even know the self I utter.
It is poured out forever
into silence.
It will not return.
I give it up.

Just thinking, God, how we begin
in our mothers' bodies,
begin in another, as Tom says.

Not from zero to zero, Mr. Valéry!
I'm sorry. A piece of the truth
clutched in an elegant private corner
will not do.

We begin biologically
and pursue thus to physical peak;
then the body, downward, dying, invests
what the body can bequeath
to the world it must leave,
saying hello and farewell
together.

It is brave so to serve
silence and presence, plotting
the one grafting that none
can in flesh reject.
Words, then, are things.
Words, too, are not things.
The word made flesh
means death makes language
a miracle.

To live, God, seems to contradict
living. Words balloon about us
with the breath of the dead.
No way out of the strangeness,
the estrangements,
the exile.

Back from Atlanta, my God,
remembering those tangy old friends
there, Roche and Harriet, how
they war against poverty and racism,

give me the mode of praise,
for their fire
and this present beatitude of flames
caressing a log
until its charred side
glows with fervor.
Oh the song of the twin burning!

Give it to me to go with the music
of this sap, a tune my ear must grab
on the run, outrunning itself,
leaping to become the more
that dispersing is lost to forever.

Staring into one coal in the dark grate,
I feed it as oxygen does,
the reality blazing a chain unending,
and where I am going
is where I am and started from,
and my face is warm, warm.

Let comfort be present, going
to my friends and staying; let love
answer love's kindling.

God, today I have to laugh,
expecting the cardinal
against the snow
to tell me something!

Yesterday I expected the lovely web
of tree shadow on the old carriage house
out back to speak to my condition.

For years I have stared
at messengers of nature's opulence,
fairly screaming my need, feeling
as Beethoven must have felt
composing his Hammerklavier sonata:
*I'll show you, you goddamn piano!*
*Give something up to my necessity.*

Out back a squirrel twitches
his dainty plume. The cardinal moves,
a flowering of metabolism.
World agitates here at its center,
quivers in each breeze,
records more than it understands.

Yes, I am a hog for meaning,
for the slops of a wild imagination.
I write to right, as Maria put it.
My pride is hilarious!

There's no getting around that cardinal
though, red twitching on white,
fool that I am,
living, dying,
replacing, replaced,
unending.

What I've done
mocked by what I imagine,
glimpses of highest romance
when paradise comes down—
to taunt me?

Dull head. Hours lying about me
like disordered sticks
too wet to kindle. How can I
believe in this, much less
in the life from which it arises?

I slam into the eyes of another,
the secret, unlimited land.
I jostle a crowd of failed
relationships, iced in, shriveled
and worried.

But aren't we taunted, balked
together, my God? Don't we meet
in this murky struggle, meet in presence,
in silence, in judgment, meet
in the knowledge that now joy
itself wounds?

Questing together in the new land,
we abandon our failures.
Why, I'm hungry as a child!

I must stand under judgment
if I am to wear the dress of praise.
Only such final selfhood
encounters the joy of presence
and sings back, sings forth.

No more imaginary paradises
or enemies. To move is to be violent.
To praise is to act. To act
is to bring down judgment.

Oh foolish and lovely
is my hunger for the posture of praise!
The impurity of it!
Body's praise. Ape dance.

Like a fool, I prance about my kitchen,
to tear the stillness open,
to shatter silence.

I dance upon my enemy's grave.
Blesséd be my enemy!

If *I am* is the same
as *I am judged*,

then must I wound silence
with myself,

hearing now birds scissor
the morning across cold snow,
seeing last night the moon
as chip of bone,

joining Sylvia, that other bride
of hell, being instructed
in self-destruction, entering
her black blossoming world.
*Damned, damned* she drones,
*win or lose.*

I gather up our afterbirth,
the foulest. I set my teeth.
I take my own life. Hell arises
in stern beauty, in the final cadences
of her display, her utter descent.

I do not follow but listen,
hear and am judged into presence,
testifying she exceeded herself
in that bleak thesaurus, saying:
*This is as bad as it gets.*
She said what she heard, anger and act.
Magical extreme! Be incarnate here
and be exceeded.

In the face of the sufferer, my God,
caught by surprise, is written
the lovely precise cost of hearing another.

To exceed that call as anger
is to enter the shining place
of resurrection, is to know apocalypse.

To become anger is to raise a defense
against suffering, to try to unsay it.

Anger and its disguise, depression,
are the usual weather of our lives.
We are companioned daily by a litany
of curses; we walk a ground of sullen rebukes.

But in the total surrender of the face
bidden to an inscrutable patience,
to a scandalous bearing and acceptance,
is final joy and presence.

The one who suffers says a word
like silence, holding back, holding on,
purely obedient.

God, I may never more
be mercifully manic,
fly into a glorious fit
of fabrication.

I ail. My only candor
is claustrophobic.
Haunted by awesome ignorance,
I cannot order what I know.

Still, I measure myself
against the fallen, lost, demolished.
Then must I call the simplest task
or transaction a miracle, call it good
to cook supper, to launder, to want
to eat. So am I what I can
only marvel at!

The sublime roiling chaos
against which I set a fork, a knife,
a spoon, yet amazes, though it nourish
the near dead, end in a grave.
Heavens! I'm somber enough
to be immensely funny!

I've read the grim, the frantic,
the decadent, the callous,
but can only praise what is left to sense.
I've leapt beyond myself; I perch,
teeter, blink, wipe my runny nose.
I've flown to my fate like the Dutchman.
The future must be part grace.
I am waiting.

Calling upon you
has changed me. I can bear
being what I so massively am
and cannot escape.
Gothic swells of laughter!
I can take the joke, even
delight in it.

Before our word began singing
together, simple courage
outraged me more than crime.
Fools!

Anomie so long my bittersweet
leaves me. No backward glance.
In amazement I enter a long
expenditure, that profuse investment
of joy that holds pain
in its gritted smile.
The dying sing!

Up from the grave they arise
without enemies, ghosts of pure intention.

Blesséd challenge none can meet.
Delicious error. Inviolable altar
where murderer meets murdered
and both, consumed, rise up in ashes
to assault the rain, blurred in one image,
loss.

God help those
who think God helps them!

Some days, God, I surprise
the gaunt face of my father
in the mirror,
tight, pale, shiny skin
hugging the bone,

and through my unsturdy frame
courses his sleepless ambition
to win back, timing the self against death,
the lost ground, for him
literally the land.

Recently I learned he could not look
upon another man's mutilation
after a road-gang accident.

I heard
how failing wretched
were his first young days
pitting weakness against merciless plow.

My father comes to me thus
in my face
and in bits and pieces, stories
of his hopes, terrors, humor.

I hunger for news of my father,
communion wafers
defying the myth.

This bodily weakness shames
and amuses me. A letter to David,
and I shake and pant.

So, a cup of camomile, my God!
And a good laugh on me!
Who yam what I yam.
A good lesson methinks
that it hurt to type a word.
Pushing like a clown
I go right through the paper self
I make and land back in comic dust.
Ill, my mouth full of this dust,
stumblebum and deflated balloon,
SHAME!

Dear editor, David, I labor
with my befuddled head,
apologize for not helping
this old world to get better.
Seems I am part and parcel with
its malevolence, failure, its shitty
no-count-falling-down crap.

Dear friend, it's a wonder
I can call you *dear* and *friend*.
You are dear, very, and
this world is dear, very.
The damnable cost
is going to convince me at last.

Drawn to Jesus' notion of kinship,
God, not so much a denial
as an extension of the blood.
In exile, drawn deeper within it,
against the thick red tide
of my Southernness, I pull like a desperate
swimmer to the mysterious far shore.

Uncle Frank, passionate fisherman,
at last built him a family church.
He beamed me pride and welcome, to be
part of that one body. I wanted to stay
in his scrubbed antimacassared living room,
with his photos of the dead and quick,
the cute sprouts in tremulous cliché,
my old playmate cousins,
grey and wrinkling now, too. Oh
I was shamelessly happy and nervous!

How little Uncle Frank had lost his Flora.
Her death's a dense photographic garden
beneath clean-smelling plastic,
important paper memorial.

In one of his stories, Aunt Flora
located and caught a gigantic fish
that was where it had no business being.
Telling it, he fashions a wonder
we both enter, but confesses
he never liked to eat fish, just catch'em.

So the warm blood calls; but, like Jesus,
a passionate itinerant, I'm all out
to squander the precious familial fluid.

If I cried out like the Canaanite,
would you heal me? Wasn't it
her selflessness, more than her faith,
Jesus was persuaded to reward?

She cried for her child
as I have cried for mine,
without savior,
without hope.

The hospitals bulge.
I cannot, in conscience, ask
to be healed, only that you
come into this crippling with me.

Oh the bléssed fantasies
of the Gospels!
Bright major songs
of Jesus' purity and compassion.
Bless him and all who would have
the world otherwise, who sing it
towards transfiguration.

If art is where what we would is,
give me acceptance
of an incredible promise
that what I am, broken, small, helpless,
is holy. So might I enter
misery without cavil.

In the hospital last week
I stared out my one window,

beheld the fingers
of a bare tree
strumming the changing air
for hours and hours,
lifting into light.

The burden, the duty of it!
The rooting into void.
Small, round, dun-colored birds
came and went in that grasping,
visitants as my unbelief
tests my belief,
shaming its pride,
giving it the force
of tentative sense.

I must not panic utterly!
Living the thousand coward deaths
to which my imagination consigns me.

Let me grasp, fallen back in my bed,
the yellow-bird symbol
of a good breakfast, sally forth
on rubbery knees to the little task—

it is large, large. It is the world
in a cup of coffee, saying, loves, I'm coming.

To swallow a bite of muffin
with Bonnie's apple jelly,
a quivering golden tart clear return
of lost time,

to swallow all pasts
in a gulp of present, of presence,
and to bite down into the marrow
as into a bar of lye washday soap,
cleansing the mouth of foul language
with a foul taste hiding in sweet.

Oh damn! God, damn! I've been hurled
into gorgeous irony in the heydey of illness:
how nothing lasts or is lost.

Into my hospital room loped another
glaring instance of this world's
inexhaustible wonder,
and though my body felt
the incarnation of the second law
of thermodynamics,

the pugnacious soul of me leapt
to the ramparts, set its sights,
careened into focus for this busy creature.

His very vest buttons pulsed.
Oracle beyond his knowing, his awkward
bones a vibrant geometry, a fluid
configuration grasped and escaping
all at once—
I craved to get my bit in his teeth
if but for a moment splintered
with the faithful fraud of glorious encounters.

Oh dear, my dear God, I know, I know.
In my shriveled compass, I am his utter dupe
and that of cads and cripples,
of a warped face tethered to a mop, hands
of mangled force—
Yet I despise the caution I have courted.
The wishful breeze of another's pointing
spirit has prickled my flesh to the soul,
however failing—

I will have this vagrant joy,
hug it to me like death.

God I'm depressed!

Talked today with Doctor Iceberg
on the phone. One sues for help
to such, gets knocked down as
by hitting a brick wall, the force
delivered by that frantic desire
in motion of body and soul.

I need help for one who can't
want help—diabolical impasse.
Drenched to the bone with failure,
I face his stony word: "Terminated."
Justification by washing of hands.
The done-with-it pomp and stifle!

*No hope, no hope* sings the silence.
What next? Beyond these official
appointments in death's fortress?

This feels like a last day.

When Eros makes the body sing
it is a time of danger and promise.
Self's lust to annex the honeyed
country of another? Narcissus
craving union with his image?
I'm tired of these.

Most dangerous and sweet to imagine
is the attraction of two strong natures
abruptly confounded by distance
one from the other, who, as though
some mighty portion lay like buried
treasure crying for rescue,

feel each aroused to venture into the other.
Risk, the vitality and push of it, arises
within and takes haughty measure
of the drab homeland, chafes
against the winnings and dust,
demands a ship, provisions, action.

Such motions, my God, seem delicious
and holy, for what is as glorious
as a total hunger?

Ah but the hunger is the promise!
Nothing I have or want truly belongs
to me. All lesser gods must bend
before the God of presence,
in whose light want perishes as it abides.
Hard words for the hungry!

As words go from slang
through informal
to full legitimacy in the lexicon,

so do we come slowly
to know one another, by a route
of uncertainty, until one day
we hail the word as flesh before us.

Next the decision: shall we use
or abuse this presence?

Mostly, in our linguistic poverty,
we ignore possible new entries,
too lazy to walk across the room
for help, for illumination, we let
meaning come unlinked, blur —
though not to learn new words
is to lose the old ones.

It's downright dangerous to skip
and prudent to pay attention.
In speaking slowness should be honored;
the best speakers falter.

Pentecost is actual,
a deep, steady smoldering
within dusty volumes.

Oh my hearer and obliteration,
often I wrong nature with sternest
demands, that evolution leap from its track
and shatter in Pentecostal explosions,
as though it was my human part to spurn
the clarity I seek, unframed as Blake's
Tyger, burning in the jungle. Certainly
I honor that brilliant monster, Stevens,
his sacrifice of all to art, the strophic
grandeur of his fleshly cathedral,
delivered up wholly to an amoral music
only the attuned can hear. To hear him
is to reach our limits and bless them.
It is to give up Heaven for heaven,
Grace for grace. It is to be lonely.
It is beyond everything gorgeous,
a sailing toward silence.

A walking insult to spring, I
blunder wearily on, ill, making
fatal mistakes because I'm confused,
weak, in pain, ashamed.

And one I would touch, oh ever so
softly, I fear. Deeply estranged
in this health-crazed time, I evade
helpful hints, the wisdom of feeling good.
My strongest belief is in the terrible
present case. I suspect it will take
the accumulated soul of the entire past
to save us. Capricious pluck wears thin.

A mess! My mouth runs maddog slobbering
in hectic bursts of old obsessive angers.
My wolfish desires pounce without warning,
going for the throat. I am lost to myself;
until some fellow wretch crunches down
full weight on a toe I didn't know I had,
I cannot know what foul truth
I'll scream. I need that medieval
assortment of devils, self-chartings
we have lost, as map of this gigantic
cretin that looms against cold heaven.

I don't want my food.

God I'm tired of the burden
of feeling. In dark commonality, boys,
taught not to cry, are so taught
not to feel. They may feel only anger,
be driven by it.
*Don't get mad; get even.*
Adepts at pure feeling absorb
the swelling debt owed for cruelty.
But we are getting angry;
the tribe is nervous.

In some body, stretching, tearing,
aching, terrible acts must find
response. We alone have been counted
dispensable enough for this costly trade;
we've felt without thinking,
becoming eternal victims.

Some days I can't read the newspaper
lest I take blame for all that's gone awry.
In our craziness we mother the crime
away from the criminal, grow tick-fat
on guilt, run like those Gadarene pigs
to drown self along with demons.

Paid to paint and perfume,
we cannot expiate what we are.
We must deny the myth of Mother,
that garbage dump, hold of dangerous wastes,
ready to explode.

Reading one more novel in which
women are mere functions
of male sexual need, by an artist
I respect, love even.

Dismayed, puzzled—why does he vomit
back experience, asserting
by not asserting: *This is just the way
it is?* What of how it should be?

Laid back, acquiescent, to know
himself monstrous, primitive
and powerful is thrilling. To take
is human, masculine;
only we are the main piece of plunder.

God, God? Where are you? These phony
monsters give an ailing culture
the cheap excitements it demands
in its fearful resistance to change;
they strut, are famous,
willing their nasty adolescence
upon the gullible.

Sisters, listen. To be is to assert,
to dream us better. Brothers, take,
instead of us, higher ground with us.
And my young friend, ambitious, straying,
come back to the self doubting
that made you as pure as fearless.
If you go on wrecking, sealed in savagery,
we will kill you.

New leaves flow their green
without going anywhere much.

I like it, as well the shaded
deep of Ellie. Like two leaves
moving together but alone; unlike
this in stunned recognition,
self of self, we share the currents
of air, the guarded hope of one more
spring here to scare us out of
our few remaining wits.

So much going wrong this spring,
vast waste and vaster want
and, inside us, an even vaster stupidity
we can no more deny than could Prospero
disown Caliban when Ariel departed,
straining after youth's brilliant falsity.

With obdurate truth I'm scarred
into my hurting bones. Heavy and formed,
I growl, pettish old watchdog
serving the decaying bones
of my lone finding.
Where is that smile? Misplaced
like a good old hat while my obstacle
self gets right in the way of impatient
life. Stammer a lame excuse, wave the
joggers on. Stagnate in my muddle,
a weight that matters little.

And you, Ellie?
Where are you in these shadows?

I cannot deny the leaf wraiths
invading the skeletal branches,
soft yet brazen insinuations,
like princesses out of a far romance
†

lying in silken skiffs
as though, inside the pearly skin,
all the bones were subtly broken.

God, I cannot find a sane path.
No fair form calls me into being.
I'm merely this sickness:
Emily hiding self and its issue;
Jane scurrying into hiding with
damning pen and paper;
Sylvia, out of hiding, blown flat
to the hardening wall with her dreadful
gift, its message of hurt beyond help.

Ellie, crippled with me, divided,
as the leaves we are an old newness
that proclaims itself, falls and rots.
How to escape? How to be without such
bleak declaration, go back to sending
forth the archaic message of the womb,
sew the altar cloth, shroud, nourish,
be mirror and plunder and home!

Beyond choice in this matter, out
of silence we come,
as into a temple newly rising.
We shall have faces where once
we bore mirrors. We shall be criminals.

Smug coward, I refuse to enter
this unmerciful spring.

Here with wintry scraps, reduced
and chill on the claw-hardened
floor of my chicken-coop self,
I'm the rigid fowl
no longer fooled.

Bereft of detaining manners, that
putting things off which is civilization,
beasts gobble up the creation
only part created, unleashed hunger,
false and infinitely ugly,
fact swallowing idea. Idea, a thin
crust long deriving, flakes away
now, dead paint.

Children,
blossoms born to disease, curse and scorn
what might save them; deafened by murderous
music, robbed of charity and sacrifice,
roboted by insidious slogans: *Be thin,
wash your hair, be sexy*; be anything
but responsible and responsive; heap
the altar of The Church of Weight-
Watchers and Pimps.

I know a spacious firmament of pain.
The great ghosts cower here with me,
more real than flesh. Oh God, I tell you
these wretched children are innocent!

God how she broods, this exemplary
woman, Ellie, keeps her own shadowy
counsel, quietly steers the prow
of self right into the storm.

Having a self, the heinous cost of it,
that lone guerrilla, her body, knows,
hacking through the pest-filled
jungle, trusting nobody to help her.

They will call you crazy.
They will call you drunkard,
castrater. Worst of all for a woman,
they will call you egotist.

Betrayed by their own bodies
into nest sexuality, young girls
will despise you for spoiling
the singing in their veins.
You will drink this bitterest cup.

Your sons will fear you. If you are
lucky, your husband will keep to your side
in weary, dogged justice. You will know
the infinite self-hatred
that companions certain vision.

Born half-dead, death will cling to you;
you will no longer be able to lullay
it to sleep. With Paul you will know
you are up against powers and principalities.

Every day of your life somebody
will try to kill the messenger
who brings the bad tidings:
*We have to change.*

Beneath our walking feet
upon the sidewalk, pavement, lawns,

winged seeds of the maples.

Above, Leviathan green,
annually intimate yet
infinitely strange, breathes,

assaults and caresses.

Back I go to the 18th century,
with my friend Cowper who needed a Friend
to author this plenitude,
the balancing point Butler sought.

Overcoming a melancholy they both
would understand, arising where the huge
*what is* silences the *I am*,

I find for myself in this lone now.
Oh could I be a cellular configuration
delighting a botanist
with noted swirling line or womblike
bulge, could I touch down gently
on hard concrete, escape my coded
gestation, sprouting, be stopped
as point of observation, could I be

the crackling dream in the botanist's mind,
thought's freedom, being's cross!
Cowper! Balanced imbalance.

I'm cold, with a utilitarian's
bad conscience, seeing through
the sham of my good acts.

What I have done, how can it stand
against the shrilling needs?
Haven't I spent most of my days
evading boredom, escaping duties
felt extrinsic to my desires?
How it disgusts me, being called
a poet!

Oh my children how fearfully
I have failed you! Such treachery
to have been out searching
when you needed me at your side.

Chilling failure. Hopeless.
The young foundering in confusion.
The old dying in debased ideals.

Where are the words?
In this cold silence, who fails?

Terrible skepticism mine, doubting
the skeptics, those who affirm
through vital denial.

Have I been swaggering only?
Is to act always pathetic?
Through setting my teeth, I hoped
to undo pathos. Through dogged work
I fled depression.

I disgust myself, cold
in this cold June.

Too luminous or dead
and disgusting, we certified
manic-depressives
never know a centered truth,
the firm of peace and acceptance.

Dreaming ourselves too alive,
we make insidious promises that return
to plague us when we are the inert
element with no spirit to move it.
We want to take back
all we hoped.

Before we write or speak,
we know we shall lie,
or dare we claim all experience
is Janus-faced?

Oh lovely hypocrisy, how I woo you
at my bleak festivals, the great lover
become the great hater,

where I swing in the nether arc
and learn a humor dark enough
for the bad, bad times, when the emptiest
gesture pleases because it moves at all!

Boredom my nemesis, must I be loyal
to extremes? Always lonely, hungry
for that measured sustenance the meek
inherit, can sheer rant adduce *I am?*

I have an appointment with a cigarette
on the half hour.

Neat, hospital-white
small cylinder, death as habit
taken up in compromise, enemy
and friend, my steady risk.

Who can comprehend the glamor
death always held for me,
how what survived seemed inferior?

At the end of the tragedy
comes the dull mender, resigned
cleaning woman, tired mourners,
whatever,

comes the other death.

A silence here
to match Silence.

I am freeing myself from loving,
from the push and pull
of fear and desire.

I come to you each
as abstractions:
Ben as *child*;
Glenn as *father*;
Don as *friend*.

Always the novice, I come
in ignorance to learn
your smell, contours, sounds,
with nearly the dispassion
of a machine and as limited
in response, assembly-line
eccentric.

I'd have us each worship the dead
and silence, give up all else,
leave in each other what is of no use.

The great dead do not contend
but feed us always. I pull their
weave of silence and presence about
me like a living shroud of gold.
So send me your words! When I know them
utterly in private, abstracted,
deadened to live, I shall hear your *I am*.

Who could properly sort my poisonous
dreams? I? Captain of this mutinous
crew? Clownish urchin in rags piping
to tumult and devastation?

Give me my dull habits, little good
that they are, decaying, even the hands
disobey, hesitate, forget the simplest
motions. My bones press down,
heavily dreaming toward dust.

It is long since I said goodbye
to luminous illusion and drink.
And hopefulness? I hurriedly pass
that to another before the trick
is discovered.

Damnation! The garbage of the daily
round must be protected as though
it were treasure!

I age into the true Cinderella, turning
from the bland prince to the ugly
but homey mother and sisters, finding
such terrible love in that rancor
the girl plotted to escape,

turning to the first and last injustice,
the battle over the magical beans
with Jack's suppressed brother —
the inner monster. Harvested, the beans
yield spiritual bloat.

Dreams. Tales. Escapes that lead
us back to the beginnings.

From my window the preternaturally
still green of the lilac
is an arm flung out in sleep
across the muggy day, resting
on the heavy nothing of the air.

What I wring from this silence,
twisting myself like a garment, is
a difference of air in motion
or not. On vibrant days

the aspen, marrying botany
and engineering, runs on like Chopin,
its green notes struck all at once.

Self and world I blurt. Fool!
Trilled like the aspen
or perplexed by a profound hush
like death though green.

Battling myself constantly for
health—pitiless abstraction!—

I say my dreams are my own creation,
I all the players, the props as well,
walker and tightrope,
student and resistant text.

In my do-it-myself universe, what
do I want to make? Scary.

When a child I fooled around with
bubbles for hours, messed with sticks,
leaves, acorns, rocks, corn silks—
I'd babble through the woods and fields
forever, tribal and chanting.

When bauble death arose, I forgot
lesser playthings; here was the ultimate
toy of fear and desire, the absolute glamor.

I had something then, combining play
and terror. My past is becoming
my future.

Into the silence I speak
Bill Connor, champion of muddling
through; knight errant unlikely
through the mannerless land,

he urges us, when we panic,
to simplify, patiently feel
what we feel and get on with it.

Into the hands of this psychologist
the rites have passed. He is scared
and lonely, as though called
to a high mountain and given
outrageous orders.

Soon in his sad land every bush
will be burning, as though plague
were not general, as though promises
were not mostly deferred in the keeping,
as though it were sane to be hopeful.

Considering our condition, considering
the armies of the brutal and the careless
and the needy,

his dogged believing damned well ought
to be miracle enough.

I want to feel my feelings, escape
the roboted verbal nothings,
the void of inflicted sound, enter
the forcing ground
of that strict solitude out of which
my fearful young Diane blurted:
*I want to be braver.*

When desperation seizes my blooded
nerves, muscles, bones, I want to thrash,
branches and trunk, hear
my own witch-chant, get back
to my girlhood, nails digging
into my tender palms.

Come into this house, rage;
let me pitch like a ship
in the dazzling shadow
of "ultimate waters."
Back and forth, round and round,
again, in the circling that is self
and time reduced to proscenium
for the *I am* and the *I am not.*

Bitten, I dance.
Defeated, I sing.
Stung, I drain the nectar of my enemy.

If I drown,
I drown in God.

Close to death is desire.
Tensed voyeur, I'm grateful
to my soles for hungering
after bodies.

Why should I not itch to touch
sweet breasts bobbing like fruit
upon her lean, strong bough?
Comical beauty that she is,
a-giggle with her young juices.
I imagine us, merry and drunken,
stumbling against each other
through a rollicking orchard!

And him! Mouth a ripe pucker,
tensed in thought or amusement.
I'm drawn like a vampire
to sip. His body's a compact atomizer
spraying me with merciless come-hither.
I cling to my chair, wanton
but wise, aware that these sprites
turn into trees.

And speaking of these, why are they
so erotic suddenly? I want to brush
my breasts against their dipping thighs,
lick each leaf, copulate stormily.

Even my old crippled cat
has become irresistible, urges
me into heat, nuzzling my bare foot.

Lust. Pure lust, by God!

Job's comforter, I bought
and presented the hapless flowers
to the house of the murdered son.

His mother's wrists, as though broken, ended
in limp fingers careless
with the roses, their rare salmon color;
she dumped them into the vase
to find their own order.

Alice and Jack weather assaults of memory,
time become a stage upon which
a few horrific scenes play and replay
between curtains of work, jittery diversions.

Speaking my love only reminds
of their love for him.
Shutting my mouth only leaves
them to silence
and lone humiliation,

for when one of us murders
it humiliates us all;
we scramble after excuses
for being human.

How his unknown murderer
has become our intimate!

Time, a mutilated beggar, malingers.
There is this amazing exchange
between these canceled parents:
They switch the roles of medic and fallen,
keep him alive by alternating
in themselves the guise of dying.

Never has silence wooed me more.
Never have my hands felt emptier of gift.

In makeshift prayer,
upon my clean sheet of white paper,
I dare burn words,
dare hope those wrists
will grow capable again.

Agony that is dream,
dream that is agony,

the sealed coffins burst
and back come the dead.

I say it was a dream,
but am I the dry eyes
or am I the watcher
before these relentless resurrections,
who never stops weeping?

I watch now her damnable suffering.
Awake. My heart a loathsome safe
where I hide my treasure of killed hurts.

The diamond point of her angry grief
picks at the lock.

I dream up a murderer
who runs a clean business,
takes parents with child,
seals them in silence
forever, together.

Shattered by presence,
I bow to dull daily caring, to hope
that can't sing but plugs ahead,
too tired and dusty for the name.
Hell, what is hope?
A great interminable foolishness?

In this insufferable audience
her grief jostles mine.
I put her upon the stage,
give her noble parts to play.

My love for her feels murderous.

God, how I long to separate
from the utterance
this ragged utterer,

long for pure saying,
union of presence and silence
figured in a body not my own.

This self-disowning
is why we love dead authors—
no chancing upon the sayer
proving another so like
I'd be unable to breathe
a saving difference;

for I think we hunger
after the unlike
as well as the unlikely,

in our soulless romancing
of souls, our nuptial snares
to trap presence;

for you don't appear
except as we are not,
as we court silence in the other,
turning upon that old enemy
with unutterable desire.

*Soul.* A word, an opacity.
*Self.* Another word and sentinel,
lover, weapon, the one way
who is the only way,
flesh that utters
the word made flesh,
that in being said
claims and disowns at once.

Time could be eternity's makeshift.

Far faint bird I caught
this morning,

can I bear hearing it again? Flinching,
cowering here? Can I greet
the shuddering sweats, the sights
too horrific for any eyes?

Ashamed of my deformities, open sores,
bungling hands, shuffling gait—
I should help somebody?

I'd have left long since
except for these monsters of suffering,
who deserve my mirroring self
set before their shameless continuing
in spite of, in spite of. . .

Dumped into bed each night
this carcass, little abler
than just needful to haul
its own sludge across
the criminal expanse of a day!

I, the needy, pouring out
what I don't have. I, the leper,
loving, beloved in my turn,
trying not to waste it.

"In every ordered state, wealth
is a sacred thing;
in democracies it is the only
sacred thing."

Thus, my God, Anatole France
in *Penguin Island*, a book—along with
*Nostromo*—our one-eyed leftists,
in the purity of their hearts,
should read. Whether uprising
in wrath against its oppressors
or fatly and ignorantly oppressing,

the self isn't a pretty sight.

Here, where democracy has taken,
success is counted only in dollars
and the greatest failure
is to find oneself poor.
Isn't the thief only trying
to be a good democrat?

The anti-Capitalist? Isn't power
his wealth? Nothing saves from the jinx
of resource, the brutal and tawdry
romances of getting and spending.

Choosing penury, corrupt,
insolvent, at being's extremity,

I'd like to give myself away
forever, counting it as nothing.

Still and always, God, a coward,
I watch the annual conflagration
as the trees give up their leaves,

as we, in middle age, give up our dreams
and poke among the ashes of debacle,

knowing a kindled sap once coursed
through our bodies, singing
amoral hymns, Whitman's open-throated
ramble and romp, knowing the open road
posits an exact dead end.

Damn this camaraderie of failure
and grief! Who needs this leprosy
from which the people rightly turn away?
Where went the how-to of happy? Woe
swallows wit; at the end of the sweet
party of life, sad drunks sprawl
on the cold beach, high and dry!

Who but you can enter such a mix
of disgust and pity? The iron I need
is far too suspect. The iron of mere pride
melts like butter. Since all offerings seem empty,

I think of giving my very body,
to show how little it matters—oh
for the life of a good hooker!
In a cheap hired room reeking
of disinfectant, I'd perform the rite
of self and other, purely—ha!
what a dear old romantic notion!

A dime's worth of notion to tell me
the old bod's still dear, a fitting
sacrifice. Therefore,

my grieving friends, body meets
body, grudging, insistent, aimed
though frail, there though battered.
Beautiful as flaming trees
are these fragile chalices
of our quivering bodies!

In the year's death, a loving
is born, sostenuto, as the body leaps,
as the lame shall leap, as the blind
shall see, as the mute shall sing,

as we choose through rotting teeth
our bodies, our lives.

Dear God, this day I feel
Pickwickian,
strut my belly like that illustrious
and usually affable gent

spoken in spite and jollity
and in some affection
by my dead friend I meet

in the deathless poise of pert Sam Weller,
in Jingle whose fraudulent grace I share.

This Jingle self, like Dickens' daring,
invites the world to be charmingly
diddled; while Sam—all wink and service—
leaves judgment to his betters,
presiding in godlike reservation.

Two frauds—Jingle, Pickwick—
the deliberate, the self-deluding,
live in me by turns,
twin faces of want and privilege,

my soul a politician
talking out of both sides of her mouth.

Fat or thin, two fatal poses,
I play these and many other
kinds of a fool.

But, I run off to Sam, to pure folly,
black the boots, grin and wink.

I rest in silence, trusting
what I've every reason not to,
self and all its artful dodges.

What I call my soul is one window
in a little house of light
welcoming presence.

I did not choose this window;
it chose me. I cannot steal
the window of another. If I run
from my window, judging, denying it,
there is no sighting, no presence.

*The way of the cross leads home*
goes a hymn refrain from childhood.
Destiny my crucifixion, to be one
and not many, this and not that,
mortally myself forever and ever.

To look out from here requires patience,
attention to long silences, trusting
everything! Out of silence it came;
to silence it will return. Its life
is a dialogue with silence.

Our therapists, bless them, believe
in an ally within us, a will to
health, part of us pushing for the best.

Without much knowing it, I suspect,
Bill and Maria are knights of faith,
strong, patient, reasoning
with chaos, risking much
on instinctual guesses.

Keeping to their posts in every
psychic weather, they stand at
constant attention for the rare
breakthrough, *I am* flashing forth.

Their tenderly naked faces
shine. They embarrass us,
blurting out home truths like children,

mouths agape with love to spare.
I often wonder who helps them
when they are helpless. Mostly
I think of their chosen simplicity
beneath which they have yoked
their brilliant minds, the discipline
and learning it takes to enable
one being to touch another.

Let me not run in fear from
responding self, the webs
I must spin to catch you, God,

nor from that clutch of desperation
the accepting share, and let me look
straight into the wild glance
from the deep terror of another.

Enemy or friend so met, glinting
eye to eye, except for this convention
we keep up between us, a captioned
world, a newsless reel,

we'd respond purely, in the child's
fear that makes good.

The terrible ocean braces
when gasping at the thought of
what you or I might next blurt.

What a desperate affair, this seduction
of the unseen, the unsayable,
possible creation existing both
as threat and promise.

You, my thin grieving sister, have
groped to touch my pink sweater
with your crushed fingers—so with you
I will bruise argument until
we mangle the syllables, until I grip
only your bones and hold you by force
in this terrible life.

You are one of my cherished ghosts;
others stumble at my side. Honey,
to have you blurt a chuckle
against your darkened will, why
that will keep the goddamned sun
from novaing! We rendezvous here, you,
death, me. Oh

how much I now know good death! I cozen
this personage to the table. Come to life,
Death. What a fine gourmet taste of rot!
Sprinkle, stir, fold it in, blend. Let
the tots tumble over the graves. Fugue
together wedding march and dirge. Only
buried songs resurrect. So,

Skinny, did you think your face
revealed as scaffold would enrage
me to beat you from the life
that has you gasping, retching?
Knockbones, don't you know I can
love you into death? And beyond,
into the deep bleeding soil that
ever erupts, spilling gorged saints?
Rationalist, my hands are empty, empty,

empty enough to grab you.

In this horror film on TV a crazed boy
drowned a baby in a pickle cask—

In the horror film of my remembering
babies proliferate. I dreamed this
week of getting my baby all dolled up
for the baby contest—

In the horror film a doll as lamp
replaced the drowned baby
in the bassinet; ominously the window
gaped into the wet night where barking—

In my childhood we opened our dolls' heads
soon after Christmas to get at
their eye works, boys in our fascination
with the machine—

All this I spit up, God, for your
delectation, spit up my love/hate
for babies, so easy to bruise, so forbidden
to kill; and I love this horror

because it gives a final shape
to my dull hurts; I know my spine better
when it shivers:

They come for me, too, hunched-over men
of all work with their trusty mastiffs,
smelling out my foul intentions; good men
who were babies, they ape this horror, good
at feeling what they are supposed to feel,
at doing what they ought, oh conventional
to a wonder! I could sleep with them all!
Sing them a lie-lullaby.

Stop it! In terror I cling
to the baby I rock to sleep.
†

The stove is murderous. The windows
threaten. Enter Poe. Walls drip
blood and poison. From the entrails
of the empty house I expect a shriek.

I cling and soothe the baby,
grip the lie that grips the truth.

My loves are balky, contentious,
thorny and unlikable,
hungry when I am sated, happiest
when I'm depressed, gloomy when
I want to sing and shout.

I appear at one's door as a last
resort; no answer. I think
*I've got it!*—another shoots my feet
from under me. I'm applauded;
at least one of my cherished few
reminds me of my piggishness and of how
at that very moment he is nastily oppressed.

Stranded in my pigpen, hopeless and
paralyzed, a great friend swoops down
upon me in a fit of judging neatness.
If for once I am lapping the milk of pleasure,
a helpful friend pauses to warn.

My dearest friends ask the most terrible
questions, tear the fragile fabric
of my latest plot for survival, deride
my hot affairs with presence, diminish
my pittance of courage, yawn.

In long Gethsemane they are each asleep.
I bathe their emptied faces with a gall
of tears, becoming each complexion,
understood, rejecting and rejected.

How I fail those who fail me!

Velveteen voices of classical
music announcers remind that what
soothes is distant, artificial,

while what is intimate
rasps, momently and fully engages.
My blood up, in a fury,
I meets I in the presence
of first creation.

As in facing your grief's impossible
need, my Alice, facing the shame
of my inadequacy, being but a scrap
of your wreckage, yours in the sweats

where I intersects with I—and
what went with the rest of it?

Soft, often foreign, the radio voice
disarms with its cool embrace
of the whole history of music making,

but the individual making
was a raucous stammering in God.

Obsessed with a certain hawthorn
we often drive past, how
its red berries last the winter,

this hound of horticulture
I'm wed to repeats things
as I do, only his things, keeping
us to the hard sharing that
both blesses and grates.

I'm the damned poet! But he's the one
who stalks the hawthorn, seizing
the very moment when the berry
shrivels, lamenting,

while I cavil, finding the wizened fruit
of equal interest to the plump and smooth.

In winter, he reads books on trees,
flowers, shrubs, diagrams ideal gardens,
possesses in forecast what he will never plant.

A terrible red, red hunger rides
and walks beside me, like a trusting
animal. The hunger breaks into
beatitude over the same old hawthorn,
the very one.

It is hard to quit loving,
to stop the pure gift of it;

once the pitcher is tilted,
the good milk pours on.

Called to it, commanded, I cannot
retain it. If the beloved will not
accept it, my love pours on into
the silence, sings to itself;
in wonder at itself it cavorts
like a squirrel or child,
any pretty delight.

It is sublimely final. I don't turn
back upon it, babbling trumped-up
reasons, not even when my body grows
silent, as though distant in the presence
of the beloved body. Inside me
the actual violence drums and trumpets.

Speechless before you and you, I am full
of strumming messages. Turn me inside out
and you will hear the glad world
of my unfurled billets-doux.

This plenteous planet God and I inhabit
becomes by reversal all the dark universe
beyond my unique command—

so, believe me, I will not take my love
back, never.

God, to my mother I am
an eternal four-year-old in a
poke bonnet, watering a petunia,
Hallmarked forever!

She is the genie in the bottle
against whose glass I flatten
my actual self. Genies die.

Out of an early photograph she flashes,
a girl with one arm for a book,
the other for a baby, primped, full
of piss and vinegar, queenly pious.
In the bottle the genie fluttered.

Where, God, damn-it!, is that revenue
due me, a mother, squandered
before I was born,

who shrank into the sanctimonious
and willfully ignorant postures
of 48 birthday cards celebrating
my unbirth, floral masques in pastels,
scary parade of little misses,
plump cheeks screened by bonnets.

I flinch from the silence these icons
occasion, holiness a tearing nausea
as I face the double or nothing
birth, mine and my mother's.

Will everything that rises converge?
The miracle now of Huston's movie
of *Wise Blood*, sending me back

to Flannery, the prophet who had
humor's grace. I think how Hazel Motes'
beliefs were her temptations. Inhabiting
the occasions of her being, she said
a hard *I am*, the barbs eating into her flesh,
the lye blinding. A pitiless bond
held her to the hopeless.

Gathering home the despised, the stomped-upon,
those life seems to refuse, trashes,
her wise blood amassed mystery. Hell
was her familiar hangout; she learned well
its language, customs, jokes. With Job
she was hung-up on injustice, with Kleist, too.

When all else fails, as it will,
I turn to the WANTED sign
that bears the face of this desperado.

Before the ink dries I will break
some promise. Before this day ends
I will negate most of its promising light.

So, what am I if not this perpetual onset
divorced from all possibility of happy
endings? In the beginning God:

From here I rupture void
with my perishing presence,
lay claim to that other within
the self I utter, all the not-me
woven fast by negation into what is me.

Questioning, questing, getting beyond
the linguistic trick of it as well,

bringing my words to be burnt,
not a tithe of them, all.

Forced to abandon the hope of conclusions,
the historical trick,
I cannot escape my only limit—
In the beginning God:

In such turmoil reading John's
*Vlemk!* Box of his desperate
vision, limit—I can only

bow to the mystery that leads
us plot to plot over the abused
ground, from which we make
our hapless escape in twists

of compromise. It is a vicious
business working our way out
of each realized dream.

Reading you, John, I braid our
desperations until the two harden
into a tight anonymity
of appalling strength.

At the heart of your writing
is a silence utter as snow,
you mute to whom persons and things
are entrusted, the impossible naming.
You princess, too, delivered up,
by relentless cliché demolished;
ex-poet, ex-violinist, axe-murderer,
you are each boxed dream, each desolation,

all you can garner and imagine
and the box nothing can open, too.

Last night one of my desperadoes
lectured on *Ecclesiastes*;

right out of Kafka or Dostoevsky;
I'm amazed each time we meet
he hasn't exploded into smithereens.

In this rodeo of centaurs
he rides and breaks himself.
Who could look straight into that face
where intelligence wars with anxiety,
where purity accosts passion?

As he belted out the hope
of hopelessness, I brimmed
with a stricken gratitude

for this being hurled too far
from foreclosing self;
I breathed *Amen* just in case.

Back again, to that ancient text,
to *Job* — isn't it an ambience
of bitterness fully entertained
and soundly routed?

In *Michael Kolhaus, Job*'s twin, Kleist's
masterpiece, another wounded sense
of justice answers the wounding,

only Michael finds no limit
to his fury for retribution
against an order that failed
the investment of his piety.

Reading of it, my neck hairs bristled;
the top of my head seemed to blow off,
sharing with Kleist our condition,
the arena of moral monsters.

Long before The Kant Crisis
that so bedeviled Kleist,
Job named you, God, speaking
a covenant with Leviathan
and Behemoth, breathing your breath
that kindled coals, feeling your heart
"hard as the nether millstone,"
raising you to king over all the sons
of pride, in his own pride's sorry
affliction. Yes, God, he knew you!

Well. Fully. Dreadfully. He brought
you down from that Olympian prologue —
the book's stage setting — where "God"
and "The Satan" wagered.

In the event they are one, those
two gamblers. The winnings that frame
the struggle are as stupid as bookends.

With Job I am rewarded for naming
you into anonymity, for joining
myself to that,

the naming my limit,
my means of praise.

No visionary dreaming God everywhere,
I bring you here,

taste you in my own mouth,
touch you in my own body.

I have rescued the child of me,
recovered the plenum of her idiot
dance and flowering, final advent,
continuing promise:
> *In the beginning God.*

Released from the rational monstrosity
of my dummy self, its clacking
mouth of wood,

released from the roboted doll
dancing in the frozen arena
empty of judgment and hope,

I own my wet red womb of a mouth
from which is born a blessèd babble,
a freshet entering speaking's ocean.

*Simple identity perishes in actuality.*

I speak my gladness
for the white pitcher in the window
and the green bottle,
for the rosemary's shapely tangle
crazed with silvery light;

to mute things I lend
my heavy tongue shyly, singing
into silence, as if praising.

And how fine a matter is simple lust!
The perplexity of sudden want
stinging the moment into presence.

Isn't my body another thing,
blesséd and mute, praiseworthy
and luminously proud
to await my notice and song?

Bumptious body, I adore you!
Delicious and droll, you go
your merry way in my soul's window,
full of old surprises. Bursting
with secret smiles am I, with gentle lechery

for the white pitcher that belonged
to my husband's grandmother,
for the green bottle that held wine
from California, for fresh rosemary
excellent on lamb, the plant lovelier
than a flower, for the body that makes
my body burn this week, knowing nothing
of its conquest,

for my body
both silent and singing.

This book was mainly inspired by Thomas J.J. Altizer's *The Self-Embodiment of God* (Harper & Row, 1977). While writing the poems, I also read his *Total Presence* (The Seabury Press, 1980), a book which clarifies, amplifies and deepens the earlier work.

The date heading each poem is that on which it was originally conceived.

The following are notes on specific poems.

11/2/79    The opening lines of the third stanza are from Tennyson's
(first)        *The Higher Pantheon.*

11/9/79    I refer here to Jane Austen and Joseph Conrad.

3/25/80    Here I am indebted to a poem by my friend Charles Edward
                Eaton, "Life Among the Natives" in *Colophon of the Rover*
                (A.S. Barnes & Co., 1980). In this poem Eaton writes:
                "There is something invulnerable and just
                About an honest appetite or lust—".

9/5/80      "Ultimate waters" here is quoted from Theodore Roethke's
                incomparable "Praise to the End," Part 4.

3/10/81    Here I respond to John Gardner's *Vlemk the Box Painter*
(second)    (Lord John Press, 1979).

3/18/81    This poem was inspired by a public lecture my husband,
                John Thomas Wilcox, gave on *Job*. I am also indebted
                to our friend Professor Saul Levin, classical scholar,
                for the "Olympian prologue" notion.

3/29/81    The last line of this is a quotation from Thomas J.J. Altizer.

# Index of Opening Lines

# About the Author

PATRICIA WILCOX is the editor and publisher of Iris Press in Binghamton, New York. She has authored two other collections of poetry, *Comforts of the Sun* and *A Public and Private Hearth* (Bellevue Press, 1978), and two prose works, *Shaped Notes: A Georgia Sketchbook* and *A House by the Side of the Road* (under the pseudonym E.V. Austin, Iris Press, 1975). Her husband John is a professor of philosophy at the State University of New York at Binghamton. They have three sons.

# About the Book

This is the sixth book published by Alembic Press. David Dayton designed the book, incorporating fruitful suggestions by Daniel Margulis, and composed it on a Compugraphic phototypesetter. The poems are set in eleven point Goudy Old Style with two points of leading; the dates are fourteen point Zapf Chancery Italic. The first edition, issued in both soft and hardcover, was printed on eighty pound Monadnock Caress by Art Craft of Ithaca, Inc., in August 1981.